Wheels, Wings, and Water

Fire Trucks

Heather Miller

Heinemann Library
Chicago, Illinois

© 2003 Heinemann Library
a division of Reed Elsevier Inc.
Chicago, Illinois

Customer Service 888-454-2279
Visit our website at www.heinemannlibrary.com

Designed by Sue Emerson, Heinemann Library; Page layout by Que-Net Media
Printed and bound in the United States by Lake Book Manufacturing, Inc.
Photo research by Amor Montes De Oca

07 06 05 04
10 9 8 7 6 5 4 3 2

Library of Congress Cataloging-in-Publication Data
Miller, Heather.
  Fire trucks / Heather Miller.
      v. cm. – (Wheels, wings, and water)
Includes index.
Contents: What are fire trucks? – What do fire trucks look like? – What are fire trucks made of? – What did fire trucks look like long ago? – What is a pumper truck? – What is a ladder truck? – What is a grass truck? – What is a Haz-Mat truck? – What are some special fire trucks? – Quiz – Picture glossary.
  ISBN 1-4034-0883-1 (HC), 1-4034-3620-7 (Pbk.)
  1. Fire engines–Juvenile literature. [1. Fire engines.] I. Title. II. Series.
  TH9372.M55 2003
  629.225–dc21

                                      2002014723

Acknowledgments
The author and publishers are grateful to the following for permission to reproduce copyright material:
p. 4 Bud Titlow/Visuals Unlimited; pp. 5, 6, 9 Amor Montes de Oca; pp. 7, 12, 14, 15, 22, 24 Gary Benson; p. 8 Kirk Schlea/Bruce Coleman, Inc; p. 10 Museum of History & Industry/Corbis; p. 11 Minnesota Historical Society/Corbis; p. 13 David Overcash/Bruce Coleman Inc.; p. 16 Daniel D. Lamoreux/Visuals Unlimited; p. 17 James E. Mahan/AP Wide World Photos; p. 18 Orlin Wagner/AP Wide World Photos; p. 19 Kimm Anderson/AP Wide World Photos; p. 20 Jean-Marc Giboux/Getty Images; p. 21 Courtesy of Pierce Manufacturing Inc., WI; p. 23 row 1 (L-R) Amor Montes de Oca, Gary Benson, Amor Montes de Oca; row 2 (L-R) Courtesy Dennis Wetherhold Jr., Courtesy of Pierce Manufacturing Inc., WI, row 3 (L-R) PhotoDisc, Minnesota Historical Society/Corbis, Bud Titlow/Visuals Unlimited; back cover (L-R) Courtesy of Pierce Manufacturing Inc., WI, Gary Benson

Cover photograph by George Hall/Corbis

Every effort has been made to contact copyright holders of any material reproduced in this book. Any omissions will be rectified in subsequent printings if notice is given to the publisher.

Special thanks to our advisory panel for their help in the preparation of this book:
Alice Bethke, Library Consultant
Palo Alto, CA

Eileen Day, Preschool Teacher
Chicago, IL

Kathleen Gilbert,
Second Grade Teacher
Round Rock, TX

Sandra Gilbert,
Library Media Specialist
Fiest Elementary School
Houston, TX

Jan Gobeille,
Kindergarten Teacher
Garfield Elementary
Oakland, CA

Angela Leeper,
Educational Consultant
North Carolina Department
of Public Instruction
Wake Forest, NC

Some words are shown in bold, **like this.**
You can find them in the picture glossary on page 23.

Contents

What Are Fire Trucks?

Fire trucks are **vehicles** that firefighters use to put out fires.

Fire trucks can carry people and things.

steering wheel

foot pedal

Firefighters make fire trucks go with foot pedals.

They steer with a **steering wheel**.

What Do Fire Trucks Look Like?

Fire trucks look like long **rectangles**.

Many fire trucks are red.

There are flashing lights on fire trucks.

Numbers tell which fire station the truck is from.

What Are Fire Trucks Made Of?

chrome   tire

Fire trucks are made of metal.

The shiny parts are a metal called chrome.

dashboard

The **dashboard** and **steering wheel** are plastic.

The tires are made of rubber.

How Did Fire Trucks Look Long Ago?

Early trucks looked like carts.

Firefighters pumped the water by hand.

bell

Later, **steam engines** pumped water.

Fire trucks had bells instead of sirens.

What Is a Pumper Truck?

hose bed   water tank

Pumper trucks have water tanks.

They carry hoses on a hose bed.

Pumper trucks pump water through hoses.

Firefighters hook the hoses to **hydrants** to get water.

What Is a Ladder Truck?

Ladder trucks carry ladders.

Ladders help firefighters reach tall buildings.

outriggers

A motor raises the ladder.

Outriggers keep the truck from falling over.

What Is a Grass Truck?

water tank

Grass trucks put out fires in fields.

Grass trucks carry tanks filled with water.

Grass trucks drive through grass fires.

Firefighters spray water from
the truck to put out the fire.

What Is a Haz-Mat Truck?

Haz-Mat trucks carry things used to clean up spills.

They carry special suits to keep firefighters safe.

Some Haz-Mat trucks have showers.

The showers are used to wash people who have been near spills.

What Are Some Special Fire Trucks?

Airport trucks are large fire trucks.

They are used when planes
have accidents.

driver 1

driver 2

Tiller trucks are long ladder trucks.

Two drivers must steer tiller trucks.

Quiz

Do you know what kind of truck this is?

Can you find it in the book?

Look for the answer on page 24.

Picture Glossary

dashboard
page 9

outrigger
page 15

steering wheel
pages 5, 9

Haz-Mat truck
page 18

rectangle
page 6

tiller truck
page 21

hydrant
page 13

steam engine
page 11

vehicle
page 4

23

Note to Parents and Teachers

Reading for information is an important part of a child's literacy development. Learning begins with a question about something. Help children think of themselves as investigators and researchers by encouraging their questions about the world around them. Each chapter in this book begins with a question. Read the question together. Talk about what you think the answer might be. Read the text to find out if your predictions were correct. Think of other questions you could ask about the topic, and discuss where you might find the answers. In this book, the picture glossary symbol for vehicle is a fire truck. Explain to children that a vehicle is something that can move people or things from one place to another. Some vehicles have motors, like cars, but others do not.

Index

Answer to quiz on page 22
This is a ladder truck.